Governor Tennessee.

Message of Governor John C. Brown

To the Thirty-eighth General Assembly of the State of Tennessee

Governor Tennessee.

Message of Governor John C. Brown
To the Thirty-eighth General Assembly of the State of Tennessee

ISBN/EAN: 9783337140106

Printed in Europe, USA, Canada, Australia, Japan

Cover: Foto ©ninafisch / pixelio.de

More available books at **www.hansebooks.com**

MESSAGE

OF

GOVERNOR JOHN C. BROWN

TO THE

THIRTY-EIGHTH GENERAL ASSEMBLY,

OF THE

STATE OF TENNESSEE.

Delivered Thursday, January 9, 1873.

NASHVILLE:

JONES, PURVIS & CO., PRINTERS TO THE STATE.

1873.

value of each tract of land in their district; said depositions to be taken in the civil districts where the land lies, before some Justice of the Peace of said district, by whom the depositions shall be returned to the Board of Assessors, on or before the —— day of—— in each year, and filed by them with their returns to the County Court.

" And, inasmuch as there is generally no standard of cash values affixed to lands, the value upon certain credits to be fixed by law, should first be ascertained by the Assessors from the proof, and then they should reduce it to a cash basis by a uniform rule, to be prescribed by law. No freeholder who is willing to bear his just proportion of the public burthens, in consideration of the protection afforded his life and property by the Government, can complain of this system. The testimony of his neighbors is invoked to do justice between him and the State. The same rule is applied to his neighbor. All landholders are placed upon an equality, and pay taxes in proportion to the actual value of land owned by each."

These recommendations were not adopted, and I now renew them. The reports of the Comptroller and Treasurer, now before you, demonstrate that the measures adopted instead, have failed to remedy the evils suggested, and it is evident that the whole law of assessment should be thoroughly remodeled, in order to reach a just and uniform system of assessing the entire taxable property of the State.

I still think this end cannot be attained under existing laws. The assessors should, I think, be selected from different parts of the county. They should be thoroughly identified and acquainted with the community, holding no other office, and should be appointed for a term—say of four or five years—and then be ineligible for a term.

To aid them in the discharge of their duties, and at the same time to "unearth" a large amount of personal property, especially about the towns and cities, which now pays no tax, I suggest that every tax-payer render a schedule of all his property, money, bonds, stocks, choses in action, etc., certified by him to be correct, and deliver it to the tax assessors, on or before a day specified by law, under just and proper restrictions and penalties.

This would place every tax-payer upon an equal footing. The citizen who desires to do right, will not complain at this mode of rendering his taxable property. He who is not willing to comply with the law, should be compelled to yield his obedience, so as to share equally with his fellow-citizens, the general burden.

COLLECTION OF TAXES.

While the system of assessments, for the reasons stated, is radically defective, the provisions of the law for the collection of taxes, after they have been assessed, are also inefficient, and, in some respects, inoperative.

The most important requisite of a perfect collection law is that it is so plain, certain and distinct that it cannot be mistaken, misunderstood or perverted by either the Collector or the tax payer. This being secured, the Collector should be compelled, by proper provisions and penalties, to a prompt execution of the law, and a speedy close of his trust.

Under the law, *as now administered*, too much time is allowed the Collector, within which to make his settlements, and close his account with the Comptroller.

This delay only furnishes to the Collector an opportunity for trade and speculation upon the public money, which many are not slow to embrace—always resulting in injury, and often in loss to the State. The remedy for this is plain and simply this, to allow only such time to the Collector to make his collections as may be necessary for that purpose; and so soon as that has elapsed, the Comptroller, and if necessary, the District Attorney, should be required to see that his accounts are closed at once, or take judgment at the first term, after failure, under heavy penalty. Credits are also allowed the Collector without proper guards and restrictions for lands returned for condemnation, and for supposed improper assessments and insolvencies.

To remedy this evil, I recommend that the Collector be required, upon making his returns (to the courts) to immediately notify the Board of Assessors that such returns have been made. The Board should, thereupon, within five days after the receipt of such notice, examine the returns, and if they discover that the tax assessed against any land so returned, might still be made by a sale of personalty, belonging to owner of the land, they shall direct the Collector to make such sale.

Whenever the Board shall be of the opinion that the tax, for which a credit is asked, could, by the exercise of proper diligence on the part of the Collector, have been made at any time, after the books were placed in his hands, or if the Collector should fail to make sale of personalty after being directed to do so, as above suggested, then the Board of Assessors should be required to resist and prevent the allowance of any credit to the Collector, for such taxes. If, upon examination of such returns, the assessors should find that any taxes are reported as improperly assessed, and they should find them, for that reason, uncollectable, they should rectify such assessment and direct its collection; and in default of collecting of such corrected assessment, the Collector should not be allowed any credit therefor, unless the tax-payer is insolvent.

SOURCES OF REVENUE.

The financial embarrassment of the State very forcibly suggests the necessity of seeking new sources of revenue.

The charters of our railroads exempt *perpetually* from taxation the capital stock of these corporations. Without arguing the question whether the attempt at *perpetual exemption* is in consonance with our organic law, or within the scope of legislation, it is enough to say that such power is denied by many of the ablest American jurists. The Supreme Court of Tennessee, however, leaves no room for doubt, that the exemption of the *capital stock* of a *corporation does not exempt the* SHARES OF STOCK in the corporation, in the hands of *individual stockholders.* That question was directly presented to the Court, in the case of the Union Bank against the State —9th Yerger's Reports, page 490. It is distinctly held in that case, that, although by the charter of the Union Bank, its capital stock is exempt from taxation, until the termination of its corporate existence, yet,*that the shares of stock* in the hands of individual stockholders are not thereby exempt, but such shares of stock are the subjects of taxation at their *cash value,* like other property.

This principle applies, of course, to shares of stocks held in all corporations.

You need not be reminded that under this ruling you are left without option, in taxing these stocks, under the provision of our Constitution (Article II, Section 28) providing that "all property, real, personal or mixed, *shall be taxed.*"

Since the question of taxing suits before Justices of the Peace was considered by your predecessors, and rejected because of doubts of the constitutionality of taxing litigation, the Supreme Court of Tennessee, in the case of Harrison Pepper *et al.* vs. T. I. Willis, has held that the General Assembly has the constitutional power to impose such a tax.

I now submit to you whether under the provisions of our Constitution, declaring "that taxes shall be equal and uniform throughout the State," you can tax litigation in Courts of Records, and exempt suits before Justices of the Peace. The former yields considerable revenue, and cannot be dispensed with. The latter would produce a much larger amount, and make a most valuable addition to the aggregate of our revenues, and would be a light burden upon litigants.

SALES OF LANDS FOR TAXES.

The attention of the last General Assembly was directed to the system under which lands have been sold for the collection of unpaid taxes, and I urged the necessity for the adoption of more stringent rules, in order to make such sales effective in the production of revenue. I repeat to you, what I then said:

" Your attention is invited to the fact that for many years lands sold for taxes, under section 622 of the Code, have been purchased in the name of Treasurer, as Superintendent of Public Instruction, for the use of common schools. In the majority of instances, the only result of these sales has been to charge the State with large bills of cost advanced from the school fund to pay the expenses of selling the land.

" Such lands are rarely redeemed, and the original owners are never disturbed in the possession or enjoyment of them. It is generally lands held upon speculation, or in large bodies, that are sold. This system is an immunity to those delinquents against the payment of taxes, and the honest tax-payer is the sufferer, because the deficits thus created, are made up by increased assessments against him. A large amount, perhaps many hundred thousand dollars of the revenue, remains uncollected under this law, and legislation is required, under which the lands can be re-sold, if not redeemed.

" It is recommended, also, that the section of the Code referred to be repealed, and in its stead stringent laws be enacted, by which the tax on lands, like that on personal property, may be made available to the Treasury of the State."

In addition, it is suggested that section 612 of the Code be so amended that the Tax Collector be required, in making return of lands to the Circuit Court for judgment of condemnation, to give such description of the lands returned, stating locality, boundaries and the names of owners, that a judgment of condemnation, passed upon his report, shall be sufficient to vest a valid title in the purchaser, and the Court should enforce these requirements before judgment of condemnation is pronounced. When the sale has been made, a writ of possession should be issued to the purchaser from the Court ordering the sale, and be executed without delay, and the purchaser should be allowed to hold,'use and enjoy the same, free from rent or other liability, for its proper use. The original owner, however, should have the privilege of redeeming, by paying the bid and interest, and the damages now allowed by law.

Unless this or some other stringent measure is adopted for the collection of taxes against lands, a large amount of annual assessments which should be collected, will, in the future, as in the past, be totally lost to the Treasury; and in addition, year after year, a drain will be made upon the Treasury for the costs of sales which are void. There is no reason why the owner of land should claim or receive any greater immunity from the payment of taxes, than the owner of personal property.

There is an idea, as false as it is prevalent, that the present loose system operates as a protection to the *poor man.* The poor man's land is rarely, if ever sold. It is the real estate held upon speculation, or in the hands of sharp, shrewd men, who have watched the imperfection of the law, and learned to evade it, that is generally condemned for sale. An examination of the reports of tax sales, now on file in the office of the Comptroller, will show, that in certain localities of the State, some of the largest landholders have, year after year, permitted their lands to be sold for taxes, and in this way have evaded the contribution of a single dollar to the Treasury. Each sale runs up a heavy bill of cost which must be paid out of the taxes collected from the prompt tax payer, and when paid out, is rarely, if ever, returned to the State.

This is worse than a farce, and is unjust to the good citizen who promptly meets the demand of his government. Nay, it is more; it is a flagrant violation of the letter and spirit of the Constitution.

The tax commissioners appointed under an Act of the last General Assembly to sell lands heretofore sold for taxes and purchased by the State, request an amendment to that Act, authorizing them to describe the lands (so as to identify them) in filing their bills, and that this be made to cure the defect in the original description.

EDUCATION AND COMMON SCHOOLS.

The statistics of 1870 afford the basis of a charge that Tennessee is third in ignorance of the States of the American Union. This is heralded to the world by Tennesseeans, as well as critics beyond the State, as a disgrace to our people.

Without controverting the assumed fact, let us review the condition of the State, and ascertain the causes that have retarded the growth of any educational system.

When the late civil war was inaugurated, Tennessee, with a population of 1,109,801, had a taxable list of $389,011,668.00.

At the close of the war, the assessments showed only $194,849,-387.00 of taxable property. The war had swept away $115,609,-554.00 in slaves.

And it is universally known that very little of the millions of personal property (aside from slaves), escaped the ravages of war. Meantime, the large debt owing by our people, growing out of their commercial and ordinary transactions, had swelled in volume by four or five years of accrued interest, all of which was unpaid. Tennessee, early in 1862, on account of her geographical position, became, and until the declaration of peace, continued the theatre of military operations. The school houses were closed. The country was devastated. And not until several years after hostilities actually ceased, did society attain such repose and security that schools could be re-established.

Added to this, when the people were restored to power, there was no educational fund, and the enormous public debt, already against the State, rendered it difficult to provide any permanent school fund.

A large majority of the States were free from the *actual presence of war*. All of them enjoyed seasons of immunity from the scourges that daily inflicted Tennessee throughout her borders. So that, without regard to where the responsibility for the war rests, the fact nevertheless cannot be controverted, that for a period of time, embracing the war and several years afterward, a system of schools in Tennessee was impossible.

And in 1869, when the people acceded to power, they found a State debt of nearly $43,000,000 hanging like a midnight shadow upon them. We had neither money nor credit. Our revenues were yearly absorbed in the redemption of the notes of the Bank of Tennessee and outstanding Treasury warrants. And the appalling question was, not whether we could maintain a system of common schools by the State, but could we preserve the State Government and sustain its faith and credit without bankrupting the people in their private fortunes. That problem is now happily solved. And while it is most unfortunate for the State, and especially for her children, that these untoward circumstances have paralyzed the efforts of the friends of education, yet it cannot be truthfully said that Tennessee is third in ignorance because of the indifference of her people to the subject of education. Every true son of hers, at the same time that he would aid in developing a plan to educate her children, will not fail to relieve his State from the obloquy attempted to be cast upon her fair name.

The county system, adopted more than two years since, is giving great satisfaction where its merits have been fairly tested. About thirty (30) counties have accepted its provisions. That it has defects cannot be denied by its warmest advocates. And the question is one that should not be lightly considered whether it should be abandoned, until the efficacy of amendments has been fairly applied.

If the General Assembly should determine to foster this system, I recommend that you appoint a State Superintendent, with an adequate salary, who shall devote his time exclusively to the duties imposed by that office, and if need be, an Educational Board for the State. Through their agency, the people could be awakened to the importance of testing the merits of the law, by levying a tax, and establishing schools within their respective counties. The present law might be amended, making it *obligatory* upon the county courts of the several counties, if they fail each year to levy a tax, to submit the question to a vote of the people.

Other amendments which will readily suggest themselves, upon an examination of the law, would greatly improve the county system.

After you have examined the resources of the State for revenue, and shall have matured a plan for making them available in the form of actual revenue, and shall have determined what amount will be necessary to sustain the State Government and at the same time pay the interest on the funded debt, (if you should fund it,) it will be for you then to determine whether the property of the State can sustain such an additional levy as will be adequate to the support of a system of common schools independent of or in conjunction with the county system. The fund already provided and secured by the Constitution and laws, if properly utilized, forms the foundation upon which, with the growing prosperity of the State, a system of common schools may be built up commensurate with all the wants of the State. The permanent fund is a perpetual charge upon the State, by the terms of the Constitution, and by Acts of the General Assembly annual interest is chargeable thereon, against the Treasury. In funding the debt of the State, this might be included and the payment of the interest thereon could be provided for out of the general revenue. The poll-tax secured by the Constitution, added to the annual interest on the permanent fund, would be the available sum to be expended each year.

I recommend that you memorialize the Congress of the United States to grant to Tennessee her proportionate part of the large public domain, which is being diminished every year by donations to railroads and to other corporations and to other States. If obtained, this land should be consecrated as a fund for education and common schools, under such rules and regulations as the General Assembly may prescribe, consistent with the Constitution. Whatever our preconceived ideas may be of the proper disposition to be made of the public lands, yet if we can obtain them for this purpose, it would prove a blessing to the State that no other disposition of them could accomplish.

Before leaving the subject, I beg of you to give it that attention demanded by its important influence upon the destiny of the State. The time has come when it must be met and disposed of. In governments like ours, where officers are elective by the people, too much importance cannot be attached to the education of the voter. The degree of his intelligence will be reflected in all the departments of the Government. It will manifest itself in the wisdom of our laws. Its influence will be felt in the administration of justice. It places its stamp upon society. Indeed, the prosperity and the permanency of the Government depend upon the intelligence of the people.

I only commend to you the importance of the subject, leaving to your discretion and judgment the peculiar system that should be adopted, or the improvements necessary to be made upon existing laws. Without I could anticipate your action in marshalling the resources of the State and making them available for revenue, as well as your disposition of the public debt, I cannot say more than I have already done.

The reports of the Superintendent and Warden of this institution, herewith transmitted, present the information necessary for you to estimate its condition. It is a gratifying fact that the prison has at last become self-sustaining. And when compared with the prisons of many of the States, the result we have attained is most gratifying.

In Illinois, for a period of fifteen months, the State prison was a charge on the Treasury of $130,196.52. Pennsylvania, in 1871, expended, above her receipts, $58,811.61, for her State prison. Arkansas expended in twelve months, $21,530.65, and Mississippi $23,674.35. Missouri, since 1836, has averaged $34,000.00 per annum in the deficits of the State prison. In Virginia the expenses have exceeded the income $40,000.00 per annum. In other States similar results are shown. Some of them have adopted the general leasing system, while some others farm out the prison shops, or hire the labor at a *per capita* rate.

The result in no State is so satisfactory as ours. The lessees have promptly met their obligations to the State. They have diversified the labor of the convicts, and reduced the mechanical products fifty per cent. in one year. It is to be regretted that, until the branch prisons were thoroughly organized, escapes were frequent at some of them. But it is believed that their recurrence is now effectually provided against.

The applications for pardon have been about five hundred in the past fifteen months. Each case has been carefully examined and pardons granted only where there appeared to be sufficient merit, and in a large majority of cases, where the greater part of the term had expired. The subjects of pardon have generally been cases of convictions for larceny, committed at a time when society was in a state of disorganization resulting from the recent state of war. I have found it necessary, with the increasing number of inmates, to establish and adhere to more rigid rules on this subject. The Ex-

2

ecutive is often imposed upon by these *ex parte* applications, and I have, on this account, felt constrained to protect the State, by refusing all pardons for alledged merit or hardship, until the Attorney General who prosecuted the party, and where practicable, the Judge and prosecutor, have been consulted, and afforded an opportunity to present the claims of society. It has occurred to me that some special provision should be made for juvenile offenders. It is cruel to confine a boy of tender years, say twelve or fifteen, in a felon's cell, surrounded daily by the demoralizing influences of confirmed villians, and, perhaps, for his first offense, committed, it oftens happens, under the influence of wretches who evade the law. If separate apartments, or a distinct reformatory institution could be provided for these juvenile offenders, it would be benficial to society, and more in consonance with an enlightened sentiment of humanity.

CHARITABLE INSTITUTIONS.

You will be furnished, in due time, with reports from these institutions, and at a future day of the session, I will make them the subject of special communication.

You are aware that the "Tennessee School for the Blind" having no house, has occupied, for some years past, a large building in the city at a heavy rental, and not constructed for nor well adapted to the purpose. Very recently a prominent and most worthy citizen of Nashville, in a spirit of most commendable liberality, purchased a large lot with elegant improvements, very eligibly situated in the city, and donated it, by deed, to this institution. The grounds are ample for all the purposes intended, but the building is entirely inadequate both in space and construction for the present wants of the school. The number of inmates is thirty-eight, and the demand for admission constantly increasing. The census for 1870 shows 800 as the number totally blind in the State. I submit the following extracts from one of the recent reports of the present efficient Superintendent:

"A considerable sum is now paid annually for rent. A house built for a private family always needs alteration when it is to be used for both an academy and a work-shop. All alterations and improvements in a rental building must be temporary; they are paid for by the school; they may not fully serve the purpose for which they were intended; they cannot be made without the consent of the owner; they finally benefit him, or if the material with which they are made is worth the labor of removal, it cannot be sold at cost. Moving from house to house is expensive and troublesome. All the money expended for temporary improvements is taken from funds that were intended to directly benefit the educational interests of the school, not a dollar of which can be well spared for indirect uses. These are minor considerations when compared with danger from fire and danger to life through disease.

"The blind frequently inherit scrofulous constitutions; they are generally less robust, and possess less vital energy than seeing children. In nine cases out of ten, the very causes that operated to produce blindness, prevented perfect physical development. Persons who are strong and healthy may grow stronger by exposure and fatigue; they may resist energetically the evil effects of unwholesome air, sedentary habits and continued study, but the blind are apt to sink under exposure; they soon show the injurious effects of breathing vitiated air, lack of active exercise, and close application to study; the health fails, the constitution is undermined. and death ensues. The young blind need, and ought to have, the invigorating sports of childhood more than other children, in the open air when practicable, within doors when the weather is inclement. When sleeping apartments and other rooms are crowded, ventilation is deficient; if to remedy this windows and doors are opened, chills, rheumatism, coughs, and perhaps consumption follow. The best efforts to properly regulate the supply of fresh air are often ineffectual. In 1857 the number of our pupils was almost as large as at present; we then had a commodious building, gymnasium and playground. The aid of a physician was required but twice during that year. For the past four years we had neither gymnasium nor playgrounds; our rented house (built for a single family) has been crowded, and therefore imperfectly ventilated; nearly every day a boy or girl was sick in bed, sometimes two or three at once. There was more than one severe and protracted case of illness, threatening a fatal termination. The sickness prevalent during the past four years must be, in a great measure, attributed to defective ventilation, crowded rooms and deficient exercise; for the school, in all other respects, was situated and managed as in 1857. These causes of sickness and debility might have been wholly or partially removed in a properly constructed building, surrounded with adequate grounds."

It will become necessary for you to ascertain what amount of money is requisite to utilize this munificent donation to this charity that appeals so touchingly for support. That you will generously respond I have no doubt.

CRIMINAL LAW.

It is a question well worthy of your consideration, whether a thorough revision of the Criminal Law, and especially the *Criminal Practice*, might not result in a very perceptible dimunition of the costs attending the prosecution of criminals. If a plan could be devised by which criminals could be brought to a more speedy trial, the saving would be immense in the way of jail fees and costs of State witnesses. It may well be doubted whether the provision of Section 5208 of the Code, permitting a prisoner one continuance, *upon his own affidavit alone*, that there is " too great excitement to his prejudice, to come to trial at the first term at which the case is regularly triable," is not productive of more evil than good.

Unscrupulous prisoners universally avail themselves of this provision of the section referred to, merely to gain a term, when in fact no such excitement exist.

While the prisoner should be allowed to continue, when there is too much prejudice for him to safely go to trial, yet the privilege could be guarded by requiring the affidavit of disinterested parties to the fact, and thus put it beyond the power of such unscrupulous persons to postpone their trial upon a mere personal affidavit, in cases where, in fact, no sufficient excitement exists. It is believed that such modification of the section referred to, would protect the rights of the prisoner, and at the same time prevent a large amount of cost against the State.

And, appropos to this general subject, I desire to call your attention to the question of

THE PLEA OF INSANITY IN CRIMINAL CASES.

It is a subject of extreme delicacy, but of great and increasing importance to society. It shocks every sentiment of justice to punish a human being for an act which is the result of mental derangement rather than of moral depravity. And yet, it may well be doubted whether this very sentiment is not rapidly leading to another extreme in the administration of the criminal law in American courts. Society, as well as the individual, is vitally interested, and should, by all means consistent with justice to the accused, be pro tected by the Legislative Department.

In the absence of any special legislation in Tennessee, the Supreme Court has held, under its opinion of the weight of American authorities on this subject, that in felony cases the existence of a reasonable doubt of the sanity of the accused, when the act with which he is charged was committed, entitles him to acquittal and discharge, notwithstanding the proof otherwise may be full and complete against him. It is not my purpose to discuss the soundness of this ruling, but only to call your attention to the subject and suggest the question, whether this rule, founded in extreme tenderness, for the life and liberty of the citizen, should be extended farther than cases of capital felonies; and whether in all inferior grades of offenses the plea of insanity should not be sustained by satisfactory evidence, like all other pleas.

But however you may dispose of this question, I most earnestly recommend that you require that in cases of acquittal, upon the plea of insanity, the jury shall so return in their verdict, and that it shall then be made the duty of the Court to send the accused to the Insane Asylum, only to be discharged when, in the opinion of the proper officers, all danger of a return of the malady is removed. Society demands at least this protection.

CRIMINAL PROSECUTIONS.

The great expense attending the execution of our criminal law has been often referred to by State officials, and yet the evil is not abated, but instead, the cost of criminal prosecutions is, year after year, increasing, until in some localities the amount actually paid out of the Treasury for this purpose, exceeds the entire revenue derived by the State from that locality, and we have the strange anomaly presented to us, of the crime of a community, proving a source of revenue to that community. The Comptroller's report will show an alarming increase in the cost of criminal prosecutions. It is believed that more stringent provisions for the examination of bills of cost by the officers of the Criminal Courts should be made and enforced. In other States, the system of requiring the several counties to pay the costs of their criminal prosecutions, has had a most beneficial effect, and I would urge upon the General Assembly the adoption of that system, inasmuch as it brings home to the immediate notice of the tax payers, the expense of such prosecutions, and the irregularities and impositions practiced in making up these bills of cost. The conveyance of prisoners after conviction to the penitentiary, is also attended with more cost than is necessary, and might, perhaps, be to some extent avoided by adapting the pay of officers and guards, and the rates of mileage to the cheapened mode of travel.

REWARDS FOR FUGITIVES.

It is too much the case, that officers of the State neglect to use the proper efforts to arrest parties charged with crime, and unfortunately it too often appears, that it is only after a reward has been offered that an arrest can be effected. In order to prevent the escape of criminals, I have been forced to draw largely upon the Treasury in the shape of rewards, but I have attempted to limit them to such cases only as could not be reached by ordinary process. When other means have failed to arrest fugitives from justice, I have had recourse to the plan of offering rewards without publication, and giving information of the fact to such persons only as were reliable and ready to undertake the duty of arresting the fugitive. The advertisement of a reward often defeats its object, in notifying the criminals that this additional inducement was offered for his capture, and he is thus put on his guard. Complaints are frequently made to this office of the want of dispatch and efficiency in the execution of capiases and other process for criminals. It is my duty to state the fact and leave it to your judgment to devise a remedy.

COUNTY WORK HOUSES.

The last General Assembly very favorably considered the recommendations of this system, as a means of preventing crime and economising the cost of administering the criminal law.

But the measure was not adopted. More deeply impressed now than ever of the salutary effect of a carefully prepared and well executed law, providing for the establishment by the counties of workhouses, for the punishment of misdemeanors and petit larceny, I renew the recommendation on that subject made to the 37th General Assembly.

By the establishment of a proper system of work-houses in each couuty the State might be relieved of the greater part of this burden.

More than one-third of the 740 inmates now in the State Prison are undergoing punishment for the crime of petit larceny.

I would respectfully recommend that the criminal laws be so amended as to provide for the punishment of this offense as well as others of the same grade, as well as all cases of misdemeanor, by confinement and labor in the several counties where the law may have been violated. By labor upon the public roads, bridges and buildings, the prisoners may be made to reimburse the county for the expense of their confinement, and the cost of conviction, which ought, in the first instance, to be paid out of the county revenue.

PUBLIC ROADS.

It would scarcely be possible to devise a worse system than we now have for the laying out and improvement of our country roads. Bad as the law is, it is not executed. Next to a preservation of the peace of society, there is no question in which the people of the State are more vitally interested. Many localities are dependent alone upon the common "dirt road" for their channels of trade and commerce. They can reach their schools and school houses, and their churches and markets alone, over this class of thoroughfares. In winter they are often impassable, and the farmer is denied a market for his produce when most in demand and commanding the best prices. Labor fails in this way to meet its just reward, and, in the midst of discouragement, is paralyzed. The result is produce rots on the spot where it grew, and lands are not improved and cultivated to the measure of their capacity.

The remedy lies in not only improving the law, but in affording ample facilities for its execution, and providing adequate penalties, without discretion in their visitation, against those who fail to meet its requirements.

Some of the evils might be remedied by the appointment of a Road Commissioner or Commissioners for each county, charged with the duty of having the road law enforced, and reporting its violation. If authorized by law to do so, many of the counties would, doubtless, assess a tax to sustain their roads.

TURNPIKE ROADS.

By resolution of the last General Assembly, the Act of March 12,

1860, requiring the Governor, Secretary of State and Comptroller, to sell the "State's stock" in the Turnpike roads of the State, was directed to be executed. In accordance therewith, and in the absence of any specific instructions, contained in the Act referred to, the aforesaid officers advertised for proposals to purchase.

Bids were made for some of the roads. For many of them we had no propositions to purchase. In the exercise of the discretion implied by the power conferred, we rejected all the proposals and withdrew the roads from sale, chiefly because of the inadequacy of the prices offered. And in this action, we were influenced by the consideration, that the Act conferred upon us no power to require from purchasers a guarantee, that the roads should be maintained for the use and benefit of the people of the State in accordance with the terms of the charter. We deemed it of greater importance to the State, and her people, that the roads should be preserved and improved, than that the Treasury should receive the small sums offered with the risk of losing the road. The fact should not be overlooked, that the destruction of some of the roads would promote the interests of other thoroughfares. And while there is no evidence of any sinister designs against them, the contingency should be guarded by proper legislation.

It would be far better to donate the State's interest in the turnpikes, to the several counties through which they run, with a guarantee that they may be maintained according to the provisions of the charters, than to accept the prices offered without such guarantee.

I therefore recommend that the disposition of roads be provided for in such manner, as that they shall be secured and preserved as thoroughfares of travel to the public, and with a view to their ultimate improvement.

The report of the Secretary of State will inform you how far revenue from any of these roads may be expected.

In accordance with chapter CIX of the Acts of 1871, the officers therein named, compromised the State's debt against the Carthage and Hartsville Turnpike Company, with the other creditors of that corporation at $4,000 in the bonds of the State, with the coupons of July 1, 1869, and subsequent coupons attached, besides paying the counsel fees of the State.

The minimun of compromise prescribed by the Act was $3,000.

BONDS OF PUBLIC OFFICERS.

The Supreme Court of Tennessee held last winter, in tho case of the State for the use of Terry, Walsh and others vs. Blakemore and others, that when the sureties upon an official bond had paid for the principal, an amount equal to the penalty of the bond, that they were exonerated from further liabilities, regardless of the amount of the principal's defalcation. Under this ruling, we are about losing a large amount of revenue from defaulting clerks and other revenue collectors. To remedy this evil, in the future, I recommend that all officers, who are charged with the collection of public revenue, be required to execute bond in such penalty as will certainly cover the whole amount of revenue which may come into their hands ; or, if thought best, that no amount be named in the bond as penalty, but instead, that the law specially provide that the sureties shall be responsible, like their principals, for all his delinquences, no matter to what extent or amount.

And I suggest that the public interest would be greatly enhanced and subserved if this feature should be made to apply to the bonds of guardians, trustees, etc., as well as collecting and other public officers.

Before leaving this subject, I beg to suggest that when bonds of public officers are executed, and accepted by the court charged with the duty of approving them, that they become " eo instanti" a lien upon all the lands, tenements and hereditaments of the bondsmen of the same dignity, force and effect as regularly executed and registered mortgages, to continue until the liability created by the bond is discharged.

INSURANCE AND INSURANCE COMPANIES.

Complaints are made by our Home Insurance Companies that our laws, requiring deposits to be made by companies from other States, are oppressive. The objection urged is that, while the amount of bonds required to be deposited affords but little security to policy holders, the retaliatory laws of other States impose a great hardship upon our companies, when they propose to do business beyond the limits of Tennessee. It is urged too that the tax now imposed upon Insurance Companies operates as a prohibition to many companies to enter the State, while others are evading the law. I have not had an opportunity to give the subject sufficient investigation to make any recommendations further than to state that the deposits should either be increased or altogether abolished. It now affords but little protection.

THE CAPITOL BUILDING AND GROUNDS.

Some appropriation will be necessary to preserve the Capitol: The sashes are decaying and must soon be renewed. The furnaces in the basement are useless, and it believed that good furnaces would not only make the building more comfortable and healthy, but would tend to preserve it from the effects of moisture. Some of the stones in the body of the building, as well as the flagging and steps, are in a state of decay, and unless means can be devised to arrest this decay, much expense may be required to repair the damage.

The improvements on the Capitol grounds have progressed very satisfactorily, and should be pushed to completion as rapidly as possible. Specific authority should be conferred upon the Superintendent of the Prison, or upon some other officer, to give direction to and control the work.

The Superintendent of the Capitol has faithfully labored in the discharge of his duties, and accomplished much in preserving the public property at a reduced rate of expenditure.

AGRICULTURAL BUREAU.

This department of industry, upon which all other interests are dependent, is, at last, receiving the attention its importance demands. The Bureau, organized under the Act of the 14th of December, 1871, has entered upon its duties with a degree of zeal and energy that promises the most valuable results, not only for the immediate benefit of the agriculturalist, but in the interest of immigration and mining. They have been for some time, and are now, compiling statistics of soil, climate, population, prices of land and labor, mineral resources, etc., together with maps, which, when completed and published, it is believed will attract attention, more directly to Tennessee, than any other means yet devised for that purpose. They are affording facilities, too, for the analysis of soils and commercial fertilizers, which must result in incalculable benefit to the farmer. Their report will be laid before you during your session. Such appropriations should be made as will enable the Bureru to prosecute its labors successfully.

LABOR AND CAPITAL.

The surest means of securing an influx of labor and capital, is to adjust our finances, so that the rate of taxation may become fixed and uniform, and our credit restored, to provide good schools, to make the laws and their administration effective for the protection of life, liberty and property, and then give this information to the world in an impressive and convincing form. Capital is timid and will not seek investment in a State or Government whose credit is impaired, or whose finances are unsettled. Labor must be fostered by capital, and protected by law. Cheap land is not the only inducement to immigration. The tide of immigration will always flow to localities offering the greatest advantages of soil, climate, wages, cheap living and free education. We have the great Northwest to compete with. And although we offer higher inducements in climate, and perhaps in the price of labor, yet, in everything else, we are under disadvantages that we must surmount. I have no report yet from from the Emigration Bureau, and when it is received, I may make of this subject a special communication.

THE COTTON TAX.

The 37th General Assembly adopted a series of resolutions instructing our Senators and requesting our Representatives in Congress to introduce and support such measures during their next ses sion as would cause to be refunded, without delay, to the people of the cotton growing States, the tax imposed and collected upon cotton for the years 1865, 1866 and 1867. A bill for that purpose has passed two readings in the House of Representatives and is now before the Committee on Ways and Means. The second section of the bill provides, among other things, "That the Secretary of the Treasury of the United States, when said bonds shall have been authenticated as aforesaid, shall be authorized, and he is hereby required and directed to turn over and deliver to the several Governors, or other authorized agents of the several States and Territories herein mentioned, bonds equaling in amount the amounts claimed by the United States from tax on cotton in the several States, to-wit :   *   *   *   *   *   *

To Tennessee, $873,460.71,   *   *   *   *
to be held by said States to be refunded and distributed to the *parties who actually paid said tax*, either in full or in part ' *pro rata* ' as circumstances may require or otherwise to be disposed of as the several Legislatures may direct by law, if it shall be found impracticable to refund or distribute said several amounts as aforesaid, among the parties who actually paid said tax, with authority to the Secretary of the Treasury to use currency to pay fractions of one hundred dollars in all settlements with said States."

It is well known that the farmer seldom paid the tax *directly to the Government agent.* He generally sold his crop to the cotton buyers, at the market price *less the Cotton Tax*, the cotton buyer retaining the amount of the cotton tax out of the market value of the cotton to pay to the Revenue officers.

Then who lost the amount of the tax? Certainly the producer— the farmer. And it was upon him and not upon the factor, or buyer, that the tax operated as a burden.

You will doubtless concur with me then that the tax should be refunded to the producers.

I therefore recommend that you instruct our Senators and request our Representatives in Congress to procure, if possible, such an amendment to the bill as will secure the refunding of the tax to the producer, as least so far as Tennessee is concerned. That will remove all doubt as to the construction of the language " actually paid," and place the rights of the producer beyond hazard.

OUR FEDERAL DEBT.

The extra session of the Thirty-Seventh General Assembly, by an Act passed the 30th day of March, 1872, authorized and empowered the Executive to settle the mutual demands between the State and General Governments growing out of railroad claims. Ill health prevented me from visiting Washington City during the summer, and I therefore sent an agent, fully empowered to treat with the Quartermaster General. After a full investigation of the state of accounts, he addressed the Quartermaster General a communication, to which he received the accompanying reply, which is a denial of all credits claimed by the State, upon the ground that existing laws did not permit or authorize the allowing of such credits. This construction of the Acts of Congress placed it beyond my power to procure any settlement without further legislation. Congress was on the eve of adjourning, and nothing could then be done. When that body convened in December last, I procured the introduction of a bill in the House of Representatives, which passed its second reading and was referred to the Appropriate Committee, where it is now being considered. A copy of the Bill, with the correspondence and accompanying documents are herewith transmitted for your information, and for your further action. If the Bill is passed, as I hope it may be, there will be no difficulty in adjusting the claims without the payment of any money. No appropriation was made to pay the expenses of looking after this business, and I ordered the expenses of the agents paid out of the Treasury, believing it would meet your approval.

CONGRESSIONAL REPRESENTATION.

Under the provisions of chapter 239 of the Acts of the Forty Second Congress, approved May 30, 1872, supplemental to the General Apportionment Act, Tennessee was allowed an additional Representative in Congress, with a *proviso* that this additional Representative might be elected *to the Forty-Third Congress only, by the vote of the State at large.* It therefore becomes your duty, if you would secure this tenth Representative in future elections to re-district the State, so as to constitute ten Congressional Districts instead of nine, as they now exist.

The population of Tennessee, according to the ninth census, is one million two hundred and fifty-eight thousand, five hundred and twenty (1,258,520), while the voting population is two hundred and fifty-eight thousand and ninety-three (258,093). An exact apportionment of the aggregate of population between ten districts would therefore, give to each district one hundred and twenty-five thousand eight hundred and fifty-two (125,852) inhabitants. It is essentially your province to distribute this representation over the territory of the State, as your judgment of fairness may dictate, preserving always, of course, the integrity of counties.

THE WASHINGTON NATIONAL MONUMENT.

I respectfully transmit for your consideration, copies of Acts of the States of New York and New Jersey, with the correspondence the Governors of those States, upon this subject.

RIVER IMPROVEMENTS.

The Governors of Pennsylvania, Ohio, West Virginia, Kentucky, Tennessee, Indiana and Illinois, constituted a Commission, to devise and consider measures for the improvement of navigation of the Ohio River and its tributaries. Tennessee is vitally interested in the subject, especially so, as to the Tennessee and Cumberland rivers, and was well represented in the commission by commercial men of the State. You are requested to give this subject the consideration its great importance demands, and to unite with the Commission memoralizing Congress, in behalf of this great improvement in which the State has such large interests.

In conclusion, permit me to indulge the hope that your deliberations may be characterized by wisdom and prudence. While all of you are animated by a desire to promote the common good, yet you may differ upon the means of reaching that end. A Compromising disposition will enable you to harmonize in results. Trusting that a sense of duty to the State may inspire such sentiments, I bid you God speed in your labors.

JOHN C. BROWN,
Governor.

EXECUTIVE OFFICE, Jan'y 9, 1873.

APPENDIX

TO

GOVERNOR'S MESSAGE.

RELIEF OF THE STATE OF TENNESSEE.
[To accompany bill H. R. No. 3000.]

PAPERS

RELATIVE TO

CLAIM FOR RELIEF

FROM

THE STATE OF TENNESSEE.

DECEMBER 3, 1872.—Referred to the Committee on the Judiciary and ordered to be printed.

EXECUTIVE OFFICE, }
Nashville, Tennessee, November 23, 1872. }

DEAR SIR: As you have just been elected a Representative in Congress, by the general vote of the State, I make free to invoke your active and earnest co-operation in securing legislation in behalf of the State of Tennessee.

You will perceive from an examination of the inclosures, that the United States Government holds three bonds, executed by Governor Brownlow the 1st of June, 1866, for $337,993.73, $94,142.85, and $21,661.73, respectively, and all bearing interest at the rate of 7 3-10 per cent. per annum. The stated account from the Quartermaster-General's office shows the credits that have been given for postal service, and the credits on that account, still to be applied, are not in dispute.

3

The proof is abundant that the property, for the price of which these bonds were executed, was purchased and placed upon the Memphis, Clarksville and Louisville Railroad, and the Edgefield and Kentucky Railroad, by the receivers of said roads, and for the owners of said roads. The State was not a party to the purchase and sale. The companies failed to execute bonds, and the General Assembly passed an Act authorizing the Governor to execute bonds to prevent the seizure and removal of the rolling-stock by the agents of the United States Government. And the Governor did execute the bonds above alluded to. The property was at Nashville when it was sold. The contract was made at Nashville, and the bond was executed at Nashville.

You will see from examination of a letter of the Quartermaster-General, addressed to an agent sent by me to Washington City, last summer, (a copy of which is herewith enclosed,) that instructions have been given to institute suits on the bonds.

The General Assembly of Tennessee, last winter, passed an Act authorizing the Governor to settle all claims with the United States Government, and I am very anxious to do so. But you will see, from the Quartermaster-General's letter, that he does not feel authorized to allow any credits except for postal service.

I think the State is entitled to abatements and credits as follows :

1st. In abatement in price of railroad material and rolling-stock, for which the bonds were executed, to the actual value of the property at the date of sale, that value to be ascertained by proof.

2d. For the value of all bridges and other property on the Memphis, Clarksville and Louisville Railroad, and the Edgefield and Kentucky road, by the United States Government.

3d. For the value of the rails, cross-ties, and other railway material, removed from the Winchester and Alabama Railroad by the authorities of the United States Government.

The justice and equity of the first proposition becomes apparent, when I assure you that the evidence is *abundant* and *reliable* that the prices affixed to the property were generally 100 per cent. above the market value. The State was not a party to the contract. The Nashville and Chattanooga road obtained an abatement of nearly 100 per cent. upon a similar purchase made at or near the same time. Other roads have obtained similar abatements. The bonds are not collectable because they have, upon their face, an illegal rate of interest. The bonds were made and signed in Tennessee. The property was at Naihville, and the contracts made there. Therefore I think the law and justice of the case is with us. Under the law, if the State cannot be made liable upon the bonds, there is no liability against her. But there is no desire to make this question. We only wish a fair and equitable adjustment.

Upon the second proposition, permit me to say that the Memphis, Clarksville and Louisville Railroad, and the Edgefield and Kentucky road, were in the hands of receivers appointed under the internal improvement laws of Tennessee, at the time they were seized by the military authorities of the United States Government. Bridges were afterward destroyed, as well as other property, by the United States authorities, and rolling-stock and other property removed and appropriated by the Government. And whether, as an original proposition, the companies of the State would or should recover anything from the United States Government, is not the question. The point is, that the State having already lost over $3,000,000 by these roads, is it not right that the credit should be allowed as against such a demand as is now made against her ? I think she ought. The claim is on file in the Department, well fortified by proof.

As to the third proposition, I must inform you that the Winchester and Alabama Railroad was in the hands of a receiver, under the internal improvement laws, at the time it was seized by the military authorities of the United States Government in 1863. This road was about thirty miles in length, and had been built only two or three years ; the track was laid of the best English rail. The military authorities having but little use for the road, took up and removed the rails, cross-ties, etc., to another road, and used them during the war, and they have never been returned, and no compensation allowed from any source. After the war, the General Assembly loaned the credit of the State to that road to purchase iron and relay their track, and to purchase rolling-stock. The road has since been sold for $300,000, and the State loses nearly $1,000,000 entirely. But before the sale the directors of the road filed their claim against the Government and proved it, and then assigned to the State, as a payment in part of their indebtedness to the State. You will find the claim, amounting to over $300,000, in the proper Department.

I can see no good reason why this claim cannot or should not be allowed.

To meet the objection urged by the Qurtermaster-General, I propose that an appeal be made to Congress for an enabling act, and inclosed you have a hastily drawn bill, which I beg of you to reform, (if you think necessary,) and introduce at the opening of the session in December proximo, and press its passage.

You would render a great service to the State if you could get the matter adjusted, or rather secure legislation that would result in a speedy adjustment. I will either visit Washington, or send an agent, if you think it necessary or desirable.

I have written very hastily, and without much reflection. I feel sure, however, that all the important facts are furnished. Please write me your opinion, as well as the progress of the business.

Very respectfully, your obedient servant,

JNO. C. BROWN,
Governor.

Hon. HORACE MAYNARD,
Knoxville, Tennessee.

QUARTERMASTER-GENERAL'S OFFICE, }
Washington, D. C., July 3, 1872. }

SIR: In reply to your letter of the 28th ultimo, I have to state that the State of Tennessee is indebted to the United State for rolling-stock and railway material, purchased in 1865 for the Memphis, Clarksville and Louisville Railroad, in the sum of $454,613.37, and for rolling-stock and railway material, purchased for the Edgefield and Kentucky Railroad, $170,481.81, making the total due July 1, 1872, $625,095.18.

These debts were incurred by the receivers for the State of the respective roads, Mr. George T. Lewis being the purchaser, receiver, and purchasing for the Memphis, Clarksville and Louisville Railroad, and Mr. R. B. Cheatham being the receiver, and purchasing for the Edgefield and Kentucky Railroad. The property was sold the State for those roads, and to other roads in Tennessee and elsewhere, under the provisions and upon the conditions of Executive orders of August 8 and October 14, 1865. Copies inclosed.

Bonds were executed by the Governor of the State, under the express authority of the Legislature thereof for the payment of the debts. Copies inclosed.

I inclose, as requested, statements of the accounts with the roads above named to July 1, 1872, showing the debts and credits.

The Memphis, Clarksville and Louisville Railroad has presented a claim against the United States for use of road and property taken and destroyed during the war, amounting to $232,166.48. The Edgefield and Kentucky Railroad has presented no claim, but is understood to have one.

The claim of the Memphis, Clarksville and Louisville Railroad has been disallowed by this office for the reason that the road and property belonging to it were captured from a public enemy, and thereupon became the property of the United States, so as to relieve it from all charges for its use and destruction. See Acts of August 6, 1861, July 17, 1862, and March 12, 1863, and for the further reason, that payment for use of such property is prohibited by law. See Acts of July 4th, 1864, and February 21st, 1867, and Acts above named. The above furnishes, I believe, all the information specifically called for in relation to the two roads in your letter, but I desire to add that the debts are now more than four years past due, and yet no provision has been made, so far as this office is informed, for their payment. This Department is specifically charged by the Secretary of War with the collection of the amount due. The bonds also require payment to be made to the Quartermaster's Department. I shall therefore be pleased if the Governor will provide for the early payment of the debts. Papers have been prepared and submitted to the Attorney-General for the purpose of instituting suit against the State to recover the amount.

One of the conditions upon which the property was sold is that the postal earnings shall be applied to the liquidation of the debt. To carry it out the Post-Office Department requires that an agent shall be appointed by proper authority to give drafts or orders in favor of the Quartermaster's Department for the amount due and to become due. The requirement in the case of the Memphis, Clarksville and Louisville Railroad has been complied with, and credits properly made, but in the case of the Edgefield and Kentucky Railroad it has not been complied with since 1867 ; there is, therefore, four and one-half year's postal pay due that road uncredited.   I suggest that the Governor designate some person as required by the inclosed circular for that pupose, and that the person so appointed give Major M. I. Ludington, Quartermaster, United States Army, an order on the Postmaster-General for the amount due, (the amount need not be actually stated,) that the same may be placed to the credit of the road.

There is due the United States from the McMinnville and Manchester Railroad Company $70,332.86.   Suit is pending against the Company to recover the amount.

The United States have no claims against the State of Tennessee, except those mentioned above for purchases of railway material.

I shall be pleased to furnish you at any time any further information you may desire.

Very respectfully, your obedient servant,

—— ——,

Quartermaster-General, Brevet Major-General U. S. Army.

Hon. AND. B. MARTIN,

Grand Central Hotel, New York City.

IX.

The Edgefield and Kentucky Railroad Company, in account with the United States, for railway material purchased under Executive orders.

DR.

November 30, 1865, to purchases...........................	$114,772 86
June 30, 1872, interest and expenses.......................	57,574 54
	$172,347 40

CR.

October 18, 1867, by certified accounts.........	$287 12	
November 25, 1867, by certified accounts.....	21 56	
January 28, 1868, by post-office warrant......	846 22	
February 6, 1868, by post-office warrant......	360 00	
October 26, 1867, by certified accounts........	16 60	
December 5, 1867, by Treasury award.........	18 35	
November 18, 1867, by Treasury award......	315 74	
		1,865 59

June 30, 1872, by balance................................... $170,481 81

I certify that the foregoing statement is correct.

M. LUDINGTON,
Quartermaster, United States Army.

Quartermaster-General's Office,
Washington, D. C., July 2, 1872.

X.

The Memphis, Clarksville and Louisville Railroad Company, in account with the United States, for railway material purchased under Executive orders.

Dr.

November 30, 1865, to purchases.................................	$336,932	36
June 30, 1872, interest and expenses.....................	164,890	99
	$501,823	35

Cr.

May 10, 1867, by certified accounts.........	$380	30		
June 30, 1867, by certified accounts.........	52	74		
October 18, 1867, by certified accounts.....	6	93		
October 31, 1867, by cash....................	2,095	57		
November 7, 1867, by certified accounts...	22	78		
November 30, 1867, by cash..................	2,027	96		
August 4, 1868, by post-office warrant.....	11,201	43		
February 10, 1869, by post-office warrant,	2,963	26		
February 10, 1869, by post-office warrant,	100	00		
January 6, 1868, by Treasury award........	8	20		
July 22, 1868, by Treasury award...........	4	10		
June 13, 1868, by Treasury warrant........	3,973	18		
May 5, 1869, by post-office warrant.........	1,526	55		
March 26, 1869, by cash.....................	244	55		
November 12, 1869, by post-office warrant	3,073	42		
February 2, 1870, by post-office warrant...	1,536	71		
May 26, 1870, by post-office warrant........	1,546	87		
August 18, 1870, by post-office warrant...	1,546	87		
October 31, 1870, by Treasury warrant.....	180	84		
August 31, 1871, by Treasury award......	280	22		
May 31, 1872, by post-office warrant........	14,437	50		
			47,209	98

June 20, 1872, by balance....................................	$454,613	37

I certify that the foregoing statement is correct.

M. LUDINGTON,
Quartermaster, United States Army.

QUARTERMASTER GENERAL'S OFFICE,
Washington, D. C., July 2, 1872.

AN ACT

To incorporate the Tennessee and Pacific Railroad Company.

*   *   *   *   *

SECTION 57. *Be it further enacted,* That the Governor be, and he is hereby, authorized to execute a bond (for the purchase of railroad machinery, cars, and all other material purchased for the use and benefit of the Memphis, Clarksville and Louisville Railroad, from the United States military railroad Department at Nashville) to the United States.

*   *   *   *   *

SECTION 62. *Be it further enacted,* That this Act shall take effect from and after its passage.

Passed May 24, 1866.

WM. HEISKELL,
Speaker of the House of Representatives.

—— ——,
Speaker of the Senate.

I, Andrew J. Fletcher, Secretary of State of the State of Tennessee, do certify that the foregoing is a copy of so much of an Act of the General Assembly of Tennessee, passed May 24, 1866, as relates to the execution of a bond by the Governor to the United States for railroad material, the original of which is now on file in the Clerk of the Senate's office, not signed by the Speaker of the Senate, but is now the law.

In testimony whereof I have hereunto subscribed my official signature, and by order of the Governor affixed the great seal of the State of Tennessee, at the Department, in the city of Nashville, this 5th day of June, A. D. 1866.

A. J. FLETCHER,
[SEAL.]   *Secretary of State.*

True copy.

M. LUDINGTON,
Brevet Lieutenant-Colonel and Quartermaster United States Army.

BOND.

Know all Men by these Presents:

That the State of Tennessee, by the act of the Legislature of the State hereto attached, and made part hereof by Wm. G. Brownlow, Governor of the State, for and in behalf of the said State of Tennessee, does hereby acknowledge itself held and firmly bound unto the United States of America, in the full and just sum of $94,142.85, with interest thereon, at the rate of 7.3 per cent. per annum, from November 30, 1865, lawful money of the United States, for which payment, well and truly to be made to the Disbursing Quartermaster of the United States Military Railroads at his office in Nashville, or to such other Disbursing Quartermaster as may be designated by the War Department, within two years from the 30th day of November, A. D. 1865, the said State of Tennessee, by its Governor, hereby binds itself and its successors firmly by these presents.

Sealed with its great seal, attested by the signature of its Governor, and affixed by the express authority of the Legislature, this 1st day of June, in the year of our Lord 1866.

The nature of the above obligation is such that whereas the above bounden State of Tennessee, has purchased and received from the War Department of the United States, (for the use of the Edgefield and Kentucky Railroad) rolling-stock, iron rails, cross ties, chairs, spikes, timber, and other material for repairing and operating said road in quantities, at prices, and to an amount and value which shall be evidenced by the receipts given for the same by R. B. Cheatham, Receiver on the part of the State of Tennessee, to the proper officer of the War Department, upon a credit of two years from the 30th day of November, A. D. 1865, payable in equal monthly installments, with interest, at the rate of 7.3 per cent. per annum, within the said two years, either in cash to the Disbursing Quartermaster of the United States Military Railroads at his office in Nashville, or to such other Disbursing Quartermaster as may be designated by the War Department for this purpose. or in transportation of the troops or military supplies of the United States, under the orders of

the proper military authorities, at the rates of fare and tolls allowed
for such service to northern railroads; and whereas the said State of
Tennessee desires, and by these presents intends to secure to the United States, the complete and punctual payment, as aforesaid, of the
amounts which may be due for the said materials received by it from
the United States; and whereas no payments have been made, up
to the date of these presents, although large sums are due, in accordance with the terms of purchase of the materials aforesaid:
Now, therefore, if the said State of Tennessee shall well and truly
pay to the United States of America as aforesaid, within thirty days
from the date of these presents, all arrears of interest and installments due the United States upon the date hereof, to wit, the sum
of twenty-six thousand nine hundred and sixty-two dollars and fifty-
four cents, and shall thereafter pay in equal monthly installments,
either in cash or in transportation as aforesaid, to the United States,
within two years from November 30th, A. D. one thousand eight
hundred and sixty-five, then this obligation shall be void and of
no effect. But if the said State of Tennessee shall fail to pay to
the United States all or any portion of what may be due to the
United States on account of the said materials received from the
United States, within two years from November thirtieth, A. D.
one thousand eight hundred and sixty-five, either in cash as aforesaid, or in transportation as aforesaid, or shall fail to pay any of the
monthly installments aforesaid punctually when due, then this obligation shall remain in full force and effect to the extent that may
be necessary to fully repay to the United States for the full amount
which may be due on account of the said materials so received as
aforesaid, and all loss or damage which may have been incurred by
the United States, by reason of the failure of the said State of Tennessee to pay for the same what shall be due therefor, when the same
shall be due. And, as a further security for such payment and indemnity to the United States, the United States shall have a lien
upon the property sold to said State of Tennessee, and in default of
such complete and punctual payment of all moneys which may be
due on account of the aforesaid purchase of materials, be fully authorized to take possession of and sell said property, and also to
place in charge and control of the said Edgefield and Kentucky
Railroad an Agent of the said United States, who shall be fully empowered, and by these presents is fully empowered, in case of such

default as aforesaid, to collect all the revenues of the said railroad, and apply the same to the payment to the United States of all the moneys which shall be due at the times of such application of such revenues to the United States for any such material which shall have been delivered by the United States to the said State of Tennessee for the use of said railroad, or by reason of any loss or injury to the United States, resulting from such default in the payment of the same. And the said State of Tennessee shall have no authority to sell or convey out of its possession without the consent of the United States, first in writing obtained, any of the property referred to in this agreement, but shall hold and retain the same to the exclusive use of said Edgefield and Kentucky Railroad, in carrying on the business of transportation of persons and property over its line of road, until the whole is fully paid for as aforesaid.

In witness whereof the great seal of said State of Tennessee is affixed hereto by authority of its Legislature, and attested by its Governor.

WILLIAM G. BROWNLOW,
Governor State of Tennessee.

Witness:

[SEAL.]   A. S. FLETCHER,
   Secretary of State.

Know all Men by these Presents:

That the State of Tennessee, by the Act of the Legislature of the State hereto attached and made part hereof by W. G. Brownlow, Governor of the State, for and in behalf of said State of Tennessee, does hereby acknowledge itself indebted and firmly bound with the United States of America, in the full and just sum of three hundred and thirty-seven thousand nine hundred and ninety-three dollars and seventy-two cents, with interest thereon at the rate of 7 3-10 per cent. per annum, from November thirtieth, eighteen hundred and sixty-five, lawful money of the United States, for which payment, well and truly to be made to the Disbursing Quartermaster of the United States Military Railroads, at his office in Nashville, or to such other Disbursing Quartermaster as may be designated by the War Department, within two years from the thirtieth day of November, A. D. eighteen hundred and sixty-five, the said State of

Tennessee, by its Governor, hereby binds itself and its successors firmly by these presents, sealed with its great seal, attested by the signature of the Governor, and affixed by the express authority of the Legislature, this first day of June, in the year of our Lord one thousand eight hundred and sixty-six.

The nature of the above obligation is such that, whereas the above bounden State of Tennessee, has purchased and received from the War Department of the United States, for the use of the Memphis, Clarksville and Louisville Railroad, rolling-stock, iron rails, cross-ties, chairs, spikes, timbers, and other material for repairing and operating said railroad, in quantity at prices, and to an amount and value which shall be evidenced by the receipts given for the same by George T. Lewis, Receiver on the part of the State of Tennessee, to the proper officer of the War Department, upon a credit of two years from the thirtieth (30) day of November, A. D. eighteen hundred and sixty-five, payable in equal monthly installments with interest, at the rate of 7 3-10 per cent. per annum within the said two years, either in cash to the Disbursing Officer or Quartermaster of the United States Military Railroads, at his office in Nashville, or to such other Disbursing Quartermaster as may be designated by the War Department for this purpose, or in transportation of the troops or military supplies of the United States, under the orders of the proper military authorities, at the rates of fare and tolls allowed for such service to Northern railroads; and,

WHEREAS, The said State of Tennessee desires and by these presents intends to secure to the United States, the complete and punctual payment as aforesaid of the amounts which may be due for the said material received by it from the United States; and whereas no payments have been made up to the date of these presents, although large sums are due in accordance with the terms of purchase of the materials aforesaid:

Now, therefore, if the State of Tennessee shall well and truly pay to the United States of America as aforesaid, either in cash or in transportation as aforesaid, within thirty (30) days from the date of these presents, all arrears of interest and installments due the United States upon the date hereof, to-wit, the sum of ninety-six thousand eight hundred and one dollars and forty-four cents, ($96,801.44,) and shall thereafter, pay in equal monthly installments, either in cash or in transportation, as aforesaid, to the United

States, within two years from November thirtieth, A. D. eighteen hundred and sixty-five, then this obligation to be void and of no effect.

But if the said State of Tennessee shall fail to pay to the United States, all or any portion of what may be due to the United States on account of the said materials received from the United States within two years from November thirtieth, (30,) A. D. eighteen hundred and sixty-five, either in cash as aforesaid or in transportation as aforesaid, or shall fail to pay any of the monthly installments aforesaid punctually when due, then this obligation shall remain in full force and effect to the extent that may be necessary, to fully repay to the United States, for the full amount which may be due on account of the said materials so received as aforesaid; and all loss or damage which may have been incurred by the United States, by reason of the failure of the State of Tennessee, to pay for the same what shall be due therefor, when the same shall be due, and as a further security for such payment and indemnity to the United States, the United States shall have a lien upon the property sold to said State of Tennessee, and in default of such complete and punctual payment of all moneys which may be due on account of the aforesaid purchase of materials, be fully authorized to take possession of and sell said property, and also to place in charge and control of the said Memphis, Clarksville and Louisville Railroad, an Agent of the said United States, who shall be fully empowered, and by these presents is fully empowered, in case of such default as aforesaid, to collect all the revenues of the said railroad, and apply the same to the payment to the United States of all the moneys which shall be due at the times of such application of such revenues to the United States for any such materials which shall have been delivered by the United States to the said State of Tennessee for the use of said railroad, or by reason of any loss or injury to the United States, resulting from such default in the payment of the same. And the said State of Tennessee shall have no authority to sell or convey out of its possession, without the consent of the United States first in writing obtained, any of the property referred to in this agreement, but shall hold and retain the same to the exclusive use of said Memphis, Clarksville and Louisville Railroad in carrying on the business of transportation of persons and property over its line of road until the whole is fully paid as aforesaid.

In witness whereof the great seal of said State of Tennessee is affixed hereto by authority of its Legislature, and attested by its Governor.

WILLIAM G. BROWNLOW,
Governor State of Tennessee.

Witness:
A. J. FLETCHER,
Secretary of State.

Know all Men by these Presents:

That the State of Tennessee by the act of the Legislature of the State hereto attached, and made part hereof, by W. G. Brownlow, Governor of said State, for and in behalf of said State of Tennessee, does hereby acknowledge itself indebted and firmly bound with the United States of America, in the full and just sum of $21,661.73, with interest thereon, at the rate of 7 3-10 per cent. per annum, from February 28, 1866, lawful money of the United States, for which payment, well and truly to be made to the Disbursing Quartermaster of the United States Military Railroads, at his office in Nashville, or to such other Disbursing Quartermaster as may be designated by the War Department, within two years from the 28th day of February, A. D. 1866, the said State of Tennessee, by its Governor, hereby binds itself and its successors firmly by these presents. Sealed with its great seal, and attested by the signature of its Governor, affixed by the express authority of the Legislature, this the 1st day of June, 1866. The nature of the above obligation is such, that whereas the above-bounden State of Tennessee, has purchased and received from the War Department of the United States, for the use of the Edgefield and Kentucky Railroad, rolling-stock, iron rails, cross-ties, chairs, spikes, timber, and other materials, for repairing and operating said railroad, in quantities, at prices, and to an amount and value which shall be evidenced by the receipts given for the same by R. B. Cheatham, Receiver on the part of the State of Tennessee, to the proper officer of the War Department, upon a credit of two years, from the 28th day of February, A. D. 1866, payable in equal monthly installments, with interest, at the rate of 7 3-10 per cent. per annum, within the said two years, either in cash to the Disbursing officer, Quartermaster of the United States Military Railroads, at his office in Nashville, or to such other Disbursing Quartermaster as may be designated by the War Department for this purpose, or in transportation of the troops or military supplies of the United States, under the orders of the proper military authorities, at the rates of fare and tolls allowed for such service to Northern railroads; and whereas the said State of Tennessee desires, and by these presents, intends to secure to the United States, the complete and punctual payment as aforesaid, of the amounts which may be due for the said materials, received by it from the United States; and whereas no payments have been made up to the date of these presents, although large sums are due in accordance with the terms of purchase of the materials aforesaid : Now, therefore, if the State of Tennessee shall well and truly pay to the United States of America, as aforesaid, either in cash or in transportation, as aforesaid, within thirty days from the date of these presents, all arrears of interest and installments due the United States upon the date hereof, to-wit, the sum of $3,106.31, and shall thereafter pay, in equal monthly installments, either in cash or in transportation, as aforesaid, to the United States, within two years from February 28, A. D. 1866, then this obligation shall be void and of no effect.

But if the said State of Tennessee shall fail to pay to the United States all or any portion of what may be due to the United States on account of the said materials received from the United States, within two years from February 28, A. D. 1866, either in cash or in transportation, as aforesaid, or shall fail to pay any of the monthly installments aforesaid, punctually when due, then this obligation shall remain in full force and effect, to the extent that may be necessary to fully repay to the United States for the full amount which may be due on account of the said materials so received as aforesaid, and all loss or damage which may have been incurred by the United States, by reason of the failure of the State of Tennessee, to pay for the same what shall be due thereon and therefor when the same shall be due; and as a further security for such payment and indemnity to the United States, the United States shall have a lien upon the property sold to said State of Tennessee, and in default of such complete and punctual payment of all moneys, which may be due on account of the aforesaid purchase of materials be fully authorized to take possession of and sell such property, and also to place in charge and control of the said Edgefield and Kentucky Railroad an

Agent of the said United States, who shall be fully empowered, and by these presents is fully empowered, in case of such default as aforesaid, to collect all the revenues of the said railroad, and apply the same to the payment to the United States, of all the moneys which shall be due at the time of such application of such revenues to the United States, for any such materials which shall have been delivered by the United States to the said State of Tennessee, for the use of said railroad, or by reason of any loss or injury to the United States, resulting from such default in payment of the same; and the said State of Tennessee shall have no authority to sell or convey out of its possession, without the consent of the United States first in writing obtained, any of the property referred to in this agreement, but shall hold and retain the same to the exclusive use of said Edgefield and Kentucky Railroad, in carrying on the business of transportation of persons and property over its lines of road, until the whole is fully paid for as aforesaid.

In witness whereof the great seal of said State of Tennessee is affixed hereto by authority of its Legislature, and attested by its Governor.

WILLIAM G. BROWNLOW,
Governor State of Tennessee.

Witness:

[SEAL.]   A. J. FLETCHER,
Secretary of State.

QUARTERMASTER GENERAL'S OFFICE,

WASHINGTON, D. C., 28th Sept., 1865.

GENERAL ORDERS,
No. 56.

The following order, by the President of the United States, in relation to the relinquishment of the Government's control over all railroads in the State of Tennessee, and their continuations in adjoining States, now occupied by the United States military authori-

4

ties, and no longer needed for military purposes, is published for the information of all Officers and Agents of the Quartermaster's Department.

M. C. MEIGS,

Brevet Major-General, U. S. A.,

Quartermaster-General.

WAR DEPARTMENT,

WASHINGTON, August 8th, 1865.

MAJOR-GENERAL GEORGE H. THOMAS,
Commanding Military Division of Tennessee,
Nashville, Tennessee.

GENERAL:

It having been determined by the Government to relinquish control over all railroads in the State of Tennessee, and their continuations in adjoining States, that have been in charge of, and are now occupied by, the United States military authorities, and no longer needed for military purposes, you are hereby authorized and directed to turn over the same to the respective owners thereof, at as early a date as practicable, causing, in all cases of transfer as aforesaid, the following regulations to be observed and carried out:—

1. Each and every Company will be required to reorganize and elect a Board of Directors, whose loyalty shall be established to your satisfaction.

2. You will cause to be made out in triplicate, by such person or persons as you may indicate, a complete inventory of the rolling-stock, tools, and other materials and property on each road.

3. Separate inventories will be, in the same manner, made of the rolling-stock and other property originally belonging to each of said roads, and that furnished by and belonging to the Government.

4. Each Company will be required to give bonds satisfactory to the Government that they will, in twelve months from the date of transfer as aforesaid, or such other reasonable time as may be agreed upon, pay a fair valuation for the Government property turned over

to said companies, the same being first appraised by competent and disinterested parties at a fair valuation, the United States reserving all Government dues for carrying mails, and other services performed by each Company, until said obligations are paid; and if, at the maturity of said debt, the amount of Government dues, retained as aforesaid, does not liquidate the same, the balance is to be paid by the Company in money.

5. Tabular statements will be made of all expenditures by the Government for repairing each road, with a full statement of receipts from private freights, passage, and other sources; also a full statement of all transportation performed on Government account, giving the number of persons transported, and amount of freight, and the distance carried in each case—all of said reports or tabular statements to be made in triplicate, one each for the Secretary of War the Military Headquarters of the Department, and the Railroad Company.

6. All railroads in Tennessee will be required to pay all arrearages of interest due on the bonds issued by that State, prior to the date of its pretended secession from the Union, to aid in the construction of said roads, before any dividends are declared or paid to the stockholders thereof.

7. Buildings erected for Government purposes on the line of railroads, and not valuable or useful for the business of said Companies, should not form a legitimate charge against such Companies; nor should they be charged for rebuilding houses, bridges, or other structures which were destroyed by the Federal army.

8. You are authorized to give any orders to Quartermasters within your Division, which you may deem necessary to carry into execution this order.

By order of the President:

EDWIN M. STANTON,
Secretary of War.

XXII.

.

QUARTERMASTER GENERAL'S OFFICE,
WASHINGTON, D. C., Oct. 23d, 1865.

GENERAL ORDERS, }
No. 62. }

The following Order, by the President of the United States, in relation to Executive order of 8th August, 1865, extending the provisions and benefits of the same to all railroads within the limits of the Military Division of the Tennessee desiring to purchase railroad rolling stock and material from the United States, for the purpose of repairing the losses of the war, is published for the information of all officers and agents of the Quartermaster's Department.

M. C. MEIGS,
Brevet Major General, U. S. A.,
Quartermaster General.

WAR DEPARTMENT,
WASHINGTON, D. C., 14th October, 1865.

MAJOR GENERAL GEORGE H. THOMAS,
Commanding Military Division of the Tennessee,
Headquarters, Nashville, Tennessee.

GENERAL :

The provisions and benefits of the Executive Order of 8th of August, are hereby extended to all railroads, within the limits of your command, desiring to purchase railroad rolling stock and material from the United States, for the purpose of repairing the losses of the war.

You are also authorized to direct the sale to any such railroads, of rolling stock, now within the limits of your command, and not needed by the United States for actual use, upon the following conditions, if they are preferred to the terms of the Order of 8th of August, and the individual security required by you under that Order:

You will take care that this property is distributed among the several' roads according to their actual needs, and that none is sold to any railroad in excess of the reasonable requirements of its business, or to be used for purposes of speculation, sale, or hire to other roads.

You will require from all such railroad companies satisfactory bonds, in the form herewith enclosed, binding them to the payment to the United States, of the full appraised value of the property sold to them, in equal monthly instalments, with interest, at the rate of seven and three tenths per cent. per annum, within two years, credit being allowed to them, on the first of each month, for any service of military transportation rendered by them during the preceding month, at the established rates now allowed to Northern railroads for such service.

Full reports of all sales under this order will be made to the·War Department from time to time, as required by existing orders.

The serviceable railroad iron in possession of the Quartermaster's Department at Chattanooga and Nashville is excepted. It will be sold only tor cash at the prices fixed by the War Department.

BY ORDER OF THE PRESIDENT:

EDWIN M. STANTON,
Secretary of War.

BOND.

Know all Men by these Presents: That the..............................
....Railroad Company,
duly incorporated by the Act of the......................................
.............................of the State of...............................
by...its President,
acting for and in behalf of said Railroad Company, do hereby acknowledge itself and its successors held and firmly bound unto the

XXIV.

United States of America, in the full and just sum of..................
....Dollars, lawful money of the United States; for which payment, well and truly be made, to the Disbursing Quartermaster of the United States Military Railroads, at his office in Nashville, or to such other Disbursing Quartermaster as may be designated by the War Department, within two years from the date of these presents, the said railroad company, by its President, hereby binds itself and its successors, firmly by these presents:

Sealed with its corporate seal, attested by the signature of its President, and affixed by the express authority of its Directors, this ....day of....................................... in the year of our Lord one thousand eight hundred and sixty ....(186 .)

The nature of the above Obligation is such, that, Whereas, The above bounden Railroad Company has purchased and received, or shall receive, from the War Department of the United States, rolling-stock, iron rails, cross-ties, chairs, spikes, timber, and other materials for repairing and operating its railroad, in quantities, at prices, and to an amount and value which shall be evidenced by the receipts given for the same by the said railroad company to the proper officer of the said War Department, upon a credit of two years from the date of these presents, payable in equal monthly instalments, with interest, at the rate of 7 3-10 per cent. per annum, within the said two years, either in cash to the Disbursing Quartermaster of the United States Military Railroads, at his office in Nashville, or to such other disbursing Quartermaster as may be designated for this purpose by the War Department, or in transportation of the troops or military supplies of the United States, under the orders of the proper military authorities, at the rates of fare and tolls allowed for such service to Northern railroads; and,

WHEREAS, The said railroad company desires, and by these presents intends, to secure to the United States the complete and punctual payment as aforesaid, of the amounts which may be due for the said materials, received or to be received by it from the United States:

Now, therefore, If the said railroad company shall well and truly pay as aforesaid, either in cash, in equal monthly instalments, or in transportation as aforesaid, to the United States, within two years from the date of these presents, all that shall be due as aforesaid to the United States on account and in payment for all the materials received as aforesaid, from the United States; then this obligation shall be void and of no effect.

But if the said railroad company shall fail to pay to the United States, all or any portion of what may be due to the United States, on account of the said materials received from the United States within two years from the date of these presents, either in cash as aforesaid, or in transportation as aforesaid, or shall fail to pay any of the monthly instalments aforesaid, punctually when due; then this obligation shall remain in full force and effect to the extent that may be necessary to fully repay to the United States for the full amount which may be due on account of the said materials so received as aforesaid, and all loss or damage which may have been incurred by the United States, by reason of the said railroad company's failure to pay for the same, what shall be due therefor, when the same shall be due; and,

As a further security for such payment and indemnity to the United States, the United States shall have a lien upon the property sold to said company, and in default of such complete and punctual payment of all moneys which may be due on account of the aforesaid purchase of materials, be fully authorized to take possession of and sell said property, and also to place in charge and control of the said Company's Railroad, an Agent of the said United States, who shall be fully empowered, and by these presents is fully empowered, in case of such default aforesaid, to collect all the revenues of the said Company, and apply the same to the payment to the United States of all the moneys which shall be due at the times of such application of such revenues to the United States for any such materials, which shall have been delivered by the United States to the said Railroad Company, or by reason of any loss or injury to the United States resulting from such default in payment of the same. And the said Company shall have no authority to sell or convey out of its possession without the consent of the United States, first in writing obtained, any of the property referred to in this agreement; but shall hold and retain the same to the exclusive use of said Company, in carrying on the business of transportation of persons and property over its line of road, until the whole is fully paid for as aforesaid.

XXVI.

In witness whereof, the corporate seal of said railroad company is affixed hereto, by authority of its Directors, and attested by its President.

....

WITNESS :

....

NOTE.—The amount of this bond to be double the valuation of the property, sold and delivered. Internal Revenue Stamps should be affixed, to the amount of fifty cents for every thousand dollars.

IN THE HOUSE OF REPRESENTATIVES,

DECEMBER 3, 1872.

Read twice, referred to the Committee on the Judiciary, and ordered to be printed:

———— -

Mr. MAYNARD, on leave, introduced the following Bill:

A BILL.

For the relief of the State of Tennessee.

WHEREAS, the Government of the United States holds three bonds, signed by the Governor of the State of Tennessee, dated the first day of June, eighteen hundred and sixty-six, one for three hundred and thirty-seven thousand nine hundred and ninety-three dollars and seventy-three cents; another for ninety-four thousand one hundred and forty-two dollars and eighty-five cents; and the other for twenty-one thousand six hundred and sixty-one dollars and seventy-three cents, all bearing interest at the rate of seven and three-tenths per centum per annum, and payable to the United States of America, for property and railway material purchased by the Edgefield and Kentucky, and the Memphis, Clarksville and Louisville Railreads, and all of them entitled to credits for certain mail-service which is not in dispute; and

WHEREAS, the State of Tennessee claims an abatement in the amount of said bonds, and alleges as a reason therefor that the property was purchased by receivers in charge of said roads for the use and benefit of the Companies then owning them, and at extravagant prices, and said State, after the property was placed in the possession of the Companies, executed the bonds aforesaid, to prevent the stopping of said roads, by a seizure and removal of the rolling-stock from said roads by the officers and agents of the United States Government, and that, inasmuch as said Companies are utterly insolvent, and unable to pay any part of said bonds, that the State should only be charged with the actual value of the property at the date of the sale; and said State also claims credit by the value of bridges and other property of said roads destroyed while run by the United States Government; and,

WHEREAS, the said State of Tennessee claims other credits by railroad iron, spikes, cars, ties, and other property taken from the Winchester and Alabama Railroad in eighteen hundred and sixty-three, used and appropriated by the United States Government: Therefore,

Be it enacted by the Senate and House of Representatives of the United States in Congress assembled, That the Quartermaster-General of the United States be, and he is hereby authorized and directed, and required to settle with the State of Tennessee all demands between said State and the United States Government in any of its Departments; and, in doing so, he will only charge said State with the actual value of the property for which said bonds were given at the date of purchase, that value to be ascertained by proof or by the agreement of said officers and the agents of said State.

SEC. 2. That he will also credit said bonds with all property of the Memphis, Clarksville and Louisville Railroad, and the Edgefield and Kentucky Road, destroyed and not replaced and restored by the United States Government.

SEC. 3. That the said Quartermaster-General will also allow the State of Tennessee the actual value of all rails, cross-ties, spikes, chairs, and other railway material, actually removed by the United States Government from the Winchester and Alabama Railroad, and not afterward restored and replaced.

SEC. 4. That such claims as may thus be established in favor of said State will be applied as a credit on said bonds without interest, at the date of said bonds.

LAWS OF NEW YORK.

[BY AUTHORITY.]

———

[Every law, unless a different time shall be prescribed therein, shall commence and take effect throughout the State, on and not before the twentieth day after the day of its final passage, as certified by the Secretary of State. Sec. 12, title 4, chap. 7, part 1, Revised Statutes.]

CHAPTER 651.

AN ACT to make a contribution toward the completion of the Washington National Monument.

Passed April 20, 1871, by a two-third vote.

The people of the State of New York, represented in the Senate and Assembly, do enact as follows:

SECTION 1. The sum of ten thousand dollars is hereby appropriated as the contribution of the State of New York, to be paid by the Treasurer on the warrant of the Comptroller, to the Treasurer of the National Washington Monument Society, whenever the Governor shall certify that he is satisfied a sufficient sum has been subscribed from other sources to enable said Society to resume work with a reasonable prospect of completing the obelisk or shaft.

§ 2. A copy of the foregoing shall be transmitted by the Governor to the Governors of other States of the Union, with a request the they communicate the same to the Legislatures of their respective States.

STATE OF NEW YORK, } ss.
Office of the Secretary of State. }

I have compared the preceding with the original law on file in this office, and do hereby certify that the same is a correct transcript therefrom and of the whole of said original law.

HOMER A. NELSON,
Secretary of State.

STATE OF NEW YORK,
EXECUTIVE CHAMBER.
Albany, June 15th, 1871.

To His Excellency,

The Governor of Tennessee.

SIR: I transmit herewith, a copy of an Act passed at the last session of the Legislature of this State, entitled " An Act to make a contribution toward the completion of the Washington National Monument," and request that you will communicate the same to the Legislature of your State.

Very respectfully, your obedient servant,

JOHN T. HOFFMAN.

STATE OF NEW JERSEY,
EXECUTIVE DEPARTMENT,
Trenton, March 5, 1872.

His Excellency, John C. Brown,

Governor of the State of Tennessee:

SIR: Herewith I transmit copy of a law passed by the Legislature of the State of New Jersey, approved by me on the 28th day of February, A. D. 1872.

I request that you will communicate the same to the Legislature of your State.

Respectfully, your obedient servant,

JNO. PARKER.

XXXI.

STATE OF NEW JERSEY.

AN ACT TO MAKE A CONTRIBUTION TOWARD THE COMPLETION OF THE WASHINGTON NATIONAL MONUMENT.

WHEREAS, there is now standing in the City of Washington an uncompleted obelisk or shaft intended as a National Monument to the memory of GEORGE WASHINGTON; therefore, with the intent and for the purpose of completing the said Monument before the Centennial Anniversary of the Declaration of Independence,—

1. *Be it enacted by the Senate and General Assembly of the State of New Jersey,* That the sum of three thousand dollars is hereby appropriated out of any money not otherwise appropriated in the Treasury of this State, as a contribution of the State of New Jersey, to be paid by the Treasurer, on the warrant of the Comptroller, to the Treasurer of the National Washington Monument Society, whenever the Governor of this State shall certify that he is satisfied that a sufficient sum has been subscribed from other sources to enable said Society to resume work with a reasonable prospect of completing the obelisk or shaft.

2. *And be it enacted,* That a copy of this law shall be transmitted by the Governor to the Governors of other States of the Union, with a request that they communicate the same to the Legislatures of their respective States.